BORN IN THE 70s

BORN IN THE 70s

Tim Glynne-Jones

ARCTURUS

ARCTURUS

This edition published in 2018 by
Arcturus Publishing Limited
26/27 Bickels Yard, 151–153 Bermondsey Street,
London SE1 3HA

Copyright © Arcturus Holdings Limited

ISBN: 978-1-78404-745-0
AD004582UK

Printed in China

All photographs from Getty Images except for pages 38 (Topfoto) and 62 (Mirrorpix)

Contents

Introduction

The 1970s is much maligned as a decade of political strife, bad fashion, ugly architecture and dowdy interior design. Much of this is true, but it was also an age of magnificence in many respects: a decade of great music, classic TV, groundbreaking cinema and stratospheric ambition. In the context of the 20th century as a whole, the 1970s is the black sheep, the maverick, a delinquent decade, misunderstood by many but adored by those who were close to it.

It was a decade of conflicting personalities, polar opposites that sparked off each other to cause outbursts of violence and brilliance in equal measure. Freedom clashed with austerity, passivism with terrorism, broadmindedness with bigotry, and you had to decide which side you were on: Tory or Labour? Racist or Anti-racist? Punk or Ted? There was no middle ground, no third way.

This tribalism went hand in hand with the musical styles of the time. They weren't genres, they were movements. Glam rock, prog rock, punk rock, heavy metal, disco, new wave, hip-hop – each one had its followers, its fashion and its code of behaviour. It defined you, to yourself and to others. And in between them all there was Abba. Even Johnny Rotten loved Abba.

There was tribalism on the football terraces too, where the hits on *Top of the Pops* were quickly rewritten as anthems for the masses. It was not fashionable for

celebrities to declare their allegiance – rather they tried to distance themselves from what was generally seen as a hotbed of hooliganism.

The 1970s was the first decade to begin with space travel no longer a dream but a reality. All eyes turned to the stars and the future, fully expecting an age of flying cars and domesticated robots by the end of the millennium. As families huddled together for warmth by candlelight during the power cuts, or shared a bath during the droughts, they dreamed of a Utopian future of TVs in the bathroom and phones that you could take wherever you went. After all, they already had supersonic passenger jets and powdered mash!

But how would they arrive at that future? The question of the British identity as a whole was dividing the nation. It was a multicultural society and becoming more so by the day. There was no turning back from that, though some wished they could. Then there was Europe: to join or not to join? That was the question. Could Britain survive as an island, cut off from the Common Market? Or was it time to embrace our Continental cousins, especially once the old money had been decimalized in 1971?

The decades since the Second World War had seen British society develop like a growing child. First it had found its feet, then begun to explore, and then to question. The 1970s saw it exercising its rights to the full: flamboyant, brash, opinionated, offensive and challenging, but undeniably exciting and creative. It was a decade that proved that the stars shine brightest out of a pitch black sky.

When we were young

As a young child growing up in the 1970s, the world was a wild and fascinating place, full of treasures and things to explore. You could play just as your parents had played: climbing trees, building camps, riding bikes, dressing up or, in some areas where traffic had yet to intrude, playing games in the street… but you could also pretend to be a spaceman on one of the Apollo missions and build rockets out of toilet rolls and empty washing-up liquid bottles… or you could just watch TV.

By the 1970s most households had a television and some even had a colour one. As a result, more and more children were discovering the delights of established favourites such as *Blue Peter*, *The Magic Roundabout*, *Trumpton* and *Doctor Who*, along with a new wave of surreal children's programmes such as *The Clangers*, *The Wombles* and *Mr Benn*.

But too much television was not encouraged. Parents didn't want their kids to become 'square-eyed', so they were sent outside to play on their Space Hopper, or if it was raining you could sit indoors and build an Airfix model, play with your Action Man or Sindy doll, or try to master the art of Clackers.

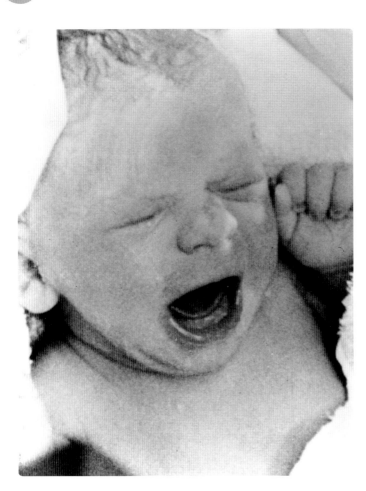

Louise Joy Brown, the world's first 'test tube' baby, photographed shortly after her birth by caesarian section at Oldham General Hospital in July 1978. The pioneering in vitro fertilization (IVF) technique sparked major concerns at the time about misusing science to create 'Frankenstein' babies and turn women into 'baby factories'.

Two cherubic siblings show the true meaning of brotherly love, a term that became well used in the 1970s, as the peace movement tried to promote its own solution to the conflict raging all around and men began to find it easier to talk about their feelings.

Five-week-old baby Emma looks slightly concerned in the hands of her dad, shot putter Geoff Capes. Capes was a British icon of the 1970s, a symbol of strength who won gold at two Commonwealth Games and two European Indoor Championships, and was crowned World's Strongest Man in 1979, all while serving in the police force.

Children gather round for a glimpse of Salome, a baby gorilla, who was born at London Zoo in 1976. Having failed to bond with her mother, Salome was nurtured by zoo keeper Ron Smith and his wife and put to bed in a cot in their home.

Prince Charles, aged 22, takes a keen interest in a sheltered housing project in Kennington, London, which forms part of the Duchy of Cornwall, of which he is duke. The nipper in the pram just wants to get indoors, by the look of it.

Two Little Boys

A hit song of the decade tells the story of two little boys who learn the value of kindness as children and grow up to bring it to bear as soldiers on the battlefield. Their toys were wooden horses, but many children re-enacted the story on any form of transport they could find to share.

In this picture the sharing is all the more poignant for the fact that the two little boys are from opposite sides of the religious divide in Northern Ireland, but sharing the same trike, the same class, the same school, the same fun, with no concept of the supposed differences between them.

Despite the peaceful desires of the majority, 'the Troubles' formed an ever-present backdrop of unease during the 1970s, both in Ulster and mainland Britain, with opposing paramilitary groups, the IRA and UVF, carrying out regular deadly bomb attacks that claimed the lives of innocent victims on both sides. Pictures like this served as a reminder that beyond the violence lay a peace-loving people that wanted to share and laugh together as one.

A 15-month-old boy looks like he's about to saddle up one of three Harlequin Great Danes – although the dog doesn't appear to be particularly onboard with the idea. The patterned cardigan and woollen hat were popular attire for toddlers in the 1970s, and indeed for many grown-ups!

It's either concentration or vengeance. The look on this girl's face is hard to read as she goes through her paces during a dance class. Girls and boys were often encouraged to attend ballet schools from a young age, while country dancing was taught in some schools.

Left *It wasn't just human babies that were enjoying the good life in the 1970s. This leopard cub looks like the cat that got the cream as she reclines to drink her daily milk in the arms of a friendly chimp at Southam Park Zoo in Warwickshire.*

Right *Undaunted by the prestige of the venue and the fact that they're supposed to be attending to the couple sauntering out through the door, a bridesmaid and page boy sneak in a quick snog while they think no one's looking during a wedding ceremony at St Paul's Cathedral.*

Opportunity Knocks

A young feminist nails her colours to the mast, possibly influenced by her mother, during a demonstration in Trafalgar Square on International Women's Day in 1973. The Women's Liberation Movement was big in the 1970s. Its demands focused on equal pay, equal education and job opportunities, free contraception and abortion and free childcare, but violence against women was also a major campaigning issue.

The movement gained strength through industrial action and other protests, including the flour bombing of the Miss World beauty pageant, and in 1975 its efforts were rewarded with three major developments: the formation of the Equal Opportunities Commission, the Employment Protection Act and the Sex Discrimination Act. Statutory maternity pay became a requirement for all employers and it became illegal to dismiss an employee for falling pregnant.

By the end of the decade Britain had its first woman prime minister, Margaret Thatcher.

The Green Cross Code man, aka actor Dave Prowse, shows children the safe way to cross the road. The Green Cross Code campaign was launched in 1970 and Prowse became a familiar sight on children's television, before going on to play Darth Vader in Star Wars.

A spaceman's helmet was the dream present for any young child in the early 1970s, as the Apollo missions brought the excitement of moon landings and returning splashdowns to our television screens on a regular basis. This little girl gets to try one on for size and finds it fits… well, just about.

Protected

. . . .

A group of children from the world's first safe house for abused women and children show the benefits of their caring surroundings. The safe house was opened by campaigner Erin Pizzey in 1971, under the name Chiswick Women's Aid, later to become the charity Refuge. Pizzey went on to open more refuges and her pioneering campaign inspired others to do the same, triggering a gradual change in social attitudes towards domestic violence. A problem that had always been kept firmly behind closed doors began to come out into the open. It was acknowledged that children needed protection from domestic violence and victims were at last given a voice.

Pizzey, herself the victim of childhood abuse from both parents, denounced the idea that domestic violence was solely a problem in men and maintained that the feminist tendency to demonize men was counter-productive to what society really needed: happy families in which children could grow up safe and secure.

Five-year-old Natalie Clarke is crowned winner of the 1973 Miss Pears contest. Her image will appear on the packaging of the famous soap brand for the next year. The Miss Pears contest was an annual attraction for aspiring young models, launched in 1958 and continuing every year until 1997.

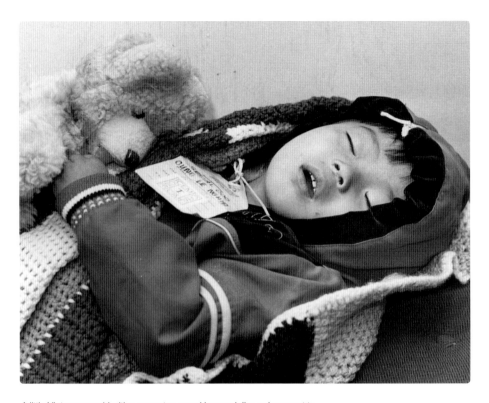

A little Vietnamese girl with a name tag round her neck lies asleep next to her teddy. After the Vietnam War ended in 1975 hundreds of thousands of refugees fled Vietnam by boat to avoid 're-education' and repression. The 'Boat People' survived storms, disease and attacks by pirates to find safe haven in the US and across western Europe.

Henry, a bloodhound who became famous in the 1970s for advertising Minced Morsels alongside the equally lugubrious writer, broadcaster and Liberal MP Clement Freud (Freud did the talking), sits before a portrait of himself as a prize-winning puppy in the company of his grandmother.

A crowd of young hopefuls bursts on to the street in London after auditioning for parts in the annual pantomime production of Peter Pan. *The production had been an annual tradition since 1904, breaking only for two years during the Second World War. But it ended in 1974.*

The early 1970s saw more children than at any other time taking school dinners. These girls are enjoying fish fingers with baked beans and potato, followed by sponge and custard. But it wasn't always that appealing. The days of semolina with jam and burnt rice pudding were by no means over.

Hopscotch grids were still a permanent fixture in playgrounds up and down the country. While boys tended to play football or cricket with tennis balls, hopscotch and skipping were the favourite playground pastimes for the girls, until they moved on to secondary school.

Children join a demonstration against the reopening of a road in Leytonstone, east London, previously closed for public safety. The days of quiet roads where children could play, safe from the threat of cars, were quickly drawing to a close. But not without a fight.

Boys and girls fly kites on a suburban street. The 1970s marked the heyday of UK Public Information Films as the state kept a benevolent eye on its children, warning them about the hazards of flying kites near electricity pylons, stranger danger, playing near open water and so on. They're dated now, but back then these films often seemed to have a sinister edge.

1971 saw the controversial scrapping of free milk in schools for children over the age of seven, an act that saw Education Secretary Margaret Thatcher dubbed 'Milk Snatcher'. For many children, though, it was not unpopular, the daily third of a pint being notoriously sour and rather hard to swallow.

Children in tank tops and Union Jack hats join a street celebration for the Queen's Silver Jubilee in 1977. The big event and a second consecutive summer heatwave saw the community spirit in abundance as the nation rediscovered a bit of national pride during what had been a difficult decade.

School's out

The old adage 'we made our own entertainment in those days' still applied in the 1970s, but kids also had a lot of new entertainment laid on. Radio stations played all the hits and every Thursday night you would sit down in front of *Top of the Pops* to see the biggest stars in music miming to their records and find out who was Number One.

Children's television took over Saturday mornings, with *Multi-Coloured Swap Shop* on BBC vying with the anarchic *Tiswas* on ITV.

Top toys of the decade were the skateboard and Rubik's Cube, both of which posed new challenges to teachers trying to keep their pupils out of harm's way and hold their attention. The government continued to grapple with the education system in an effort to provide an equal opportunity for all. The number of grammar schools declined at a rate of 90 per year and the state school system was structured into Infant, Junior and Senior schools. In 1973 the compulsory leaving age was raised from 15 to 16 in order to ensure that every child had a chance of leaving school with some form of qualification: either CSEs or the more challenging O-Levels.

You're Nicked!

A prefect frog-marches a younger pupil (who looks remarkably like he could be the older boy's brother) back to school, in a display of power that was not uncommon in the 1970s. Bullying, though frowned upon among peers, was part of the disciplinary structure applied to keep pupils in line. Becoming a prefect meant a welcome opportunity to turn some of the victimization that had come your way on to those below you.

Corporal punishment was still legal, administered with the cane, the ruler and the slipper. The latter was more commonly a shoe or plimsole – teachers rarely wore their slippers to school. Children of all ages found themselves on the receiving end whenever they stepped out of line.

1970s fashion is evident in both these characters: the shoulder-length hair, the trousers stopping several inches short of the shoes. And while the younger boy still puts up with the flappy trousers of his school uniform, the prefect has the privilege of wearing straight jeans.

Left *After years of planning, the currency of the UK finally went decimal on 15 February 1971 as pounds, shillings and pence gave way to pounds and new pence. This change had originally been suggested in 1824. Chaos ensued, with endless fumbling for change, and people kept saying, 'How much is that in old money?'*

Right *A proudly gap-toothed kid from Eccles stands before a wall daubed with the slogans of the Anti-Nazi League, an organization that formed in 1977 to combat the spread of the right-wing National Front. The political middle ground was a relative no-man's land in the 1970s.*

Left *A young ballet student shows the makings of a fine dancer during an after-school class. As the group watching shows, ballet was mostly popular with girls, but it was not unheard of for boys to attend from an early age until they developed an interest in rougher pursuits.*

Right *There's something strange about this cross-section of Arsenal fans from 1971: not a single one is sitting down and no one is wearing a replica strip. (Back then people knitted their own club crests; they'd be sued for that now.) Among matchday features of the time, please note the rosettes and sensible polo necks.*

Exuberant schoolkids full of the joys of the summer holidays in Juvenal Gardens, Liverpool. The 1970s brought a revolution in education with much flouting of convention. Up the road from here was the New Scotland Road Free School, an outpost of radicalism, where teachers often began the day by asking pupils, 'What d'yous want to do today?'

Candle in the Wind

• •

A girl lights her way to bed in the time-honoured way during a power cut in 1972. The first miners' strike for 50 years saw coal supplies dwindle to such an extent that power cuts were enforced, sometimes for nine hours a day. For children, this was a double-edged sword: living by candlelight was an exciting departure from the norm, but the lack of electricity put paid to their favourite television programmes, such as *Blue Peter*, *Jackanory* and *Magpie*.

The darkness was compounded by a return to Greenwich Mean Time in winter, following a two-year experiment in which the clocks were set forward one hour ahead of GMT throughout the year, meaning an hour's more daylight in the afternoon. Children's safety, walking home from school in the dark, became a national concern.

The power cuts lasted for three days in February 1972, until the miners' pay dispute was settled, but returned two years later as the unions went on strike again and Prime Minister Edward Heath imposed a three-day week.

A young girl in London becomes a magnet for pigeons after offering some scraps of food. Feeding the birds in Trafalgar Square was not only legal in the 1970s, it was a feature on the agenda of any visitor to the capital and the pigeons were as popular as Nelson on his column.

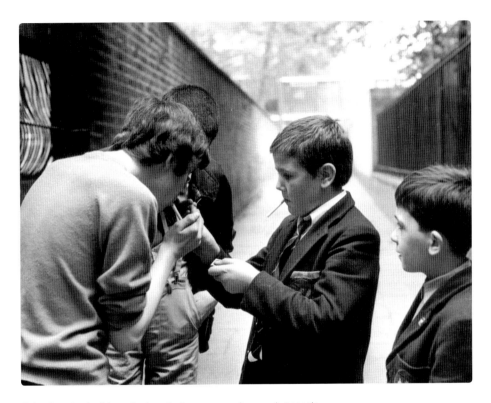

Schoolboys bunk off for a sly cigarette. It seems amazing now, but people smoked practically everywhere in the 1970s: on the top deck of buses, in cinemas, nightclubs, offices, pubs and homes, even on planes and the London Underground. Young children could buy sweet cigarettes in every newsagent's and confectioner's. No wonder they were all at it.

Two by Two

· ·

A typical classroom in a typical 1970s boys' comprehensive school. While the reorganization of the education system was designed to remove selection on the grounds of academic ability, there was still a strong school of thought that favoured separating pupils by gender, and so co-educational schools only came in slowly during the 1970s.

This picture tells you a lot about the time. Gone are the desk and chair ensembles of previous decades, the hinged lids, the inkwells. Instead it's stark, modern tables and chairs, with books kept in your bag until required. At the front of the class was still a blackboard, although whiteboards were starting to come in. While some boys wear ties, others don't – the strict disciplinary codes that had been a feature of schools in years gone by were being undermined amid the new mood of laissez-faire, which was intended to encourage kids to be more free and creative.

A group of boys from Chelsea play out their own precursor to the 1970 FA Cup Final between their local heroes and Leeds United – a clash that Chelsea would eventually win in a replay at Old Trafford. Street football was becoming an increasingly rare sight, though, as cars rapidly took over.

Two young hardnuts, one sporting the close-cropped skinhead haircut that was fashionable among young troublemakers, work hard at their intimidating stares as they queue for a football match. The football terraces were a major draw for teenage boys, with low prices and the ever-present thrill of the pack.

As the skateboard craze takes hold, competitors line up at the start of a race. Skateboarding had been around in the United States since the 1950s but the invention of polyurethane wheels and more versatile designs sparked a boom in the mid-1970s that saw every child wanting their own deck and wheels.

The go-cart, or soapbox, was a popular piece of homemade fun. All you needed was a plank of wood, a set of pram wheels from the local dump, some rope and a hill, preferably with a safe run-off area at the bottom. Any further adornments were considered a luxury.

Pupils at Harrow School assemble in the courtyard, wearing the traditional straw boaters that are part of the school uniform and compulsory attire when outdoors. As state education wrestled with the challenge of providing a more egalitarian system, independent public schools like Harrow stuck out like a sore thumb.

Above *An exam in progress at a girls' comprehensive school. Pupils in state schools usually took the Certificate of Secondary Education (CSE), which had been introduced in 1965, while those in grammar and independent schools took O-Levels. A Grade I at CSE was equivalent to an O-Level pass.*

Right *Clash T-shirt, football scarf, tartan skirt and bleached hair: two girls show they can mix it with the boys when it comes to attracting attention. Punk was a small cult movement until the appearance of the Sex Pistols on* The Today Show *in 1976 outraged the nation's parents – and delighted their kids.*

Abracadabra

· ·

One of the more unusual obsessions of the 1970s was bending spoons and forks. Not through force, you understand, but by rubbing them gently between thumb and forefinger. Many was the time mum would go to the kitchen drawer, only to find the cutlery twisted beyond recognition by some unseen force (i.e. the kids). Responsibility for this epidemic of cutlery contortion fell on the shoulders of illusionist Uri Geller, who made his first British television appearance on *Blue Peter*, bending a fork for an audience of millions of spellbound children.

He never explained how. Immediately, children throughout the country were frantically rubbing forks and spoons in an effort to make them bend. Here, magician David Berglas is inspecting contestants in a national spoon-bending contest, run by the *Daily Express*. Geller explained that he'd been given extraterrestrial powers, a claim that rubbed other magicians up the wrong way. Despite the controversy, Geller forged a successful career based on his spoon-bending 'magic'.

A crowd of schoolgirls on a day out at White City Stadium cheer on the England ladies' hockey team in a match against Australia. White City was still a major sporting venue, having been used for the World Cup in 1966, but it would not last much beyond the end of the 1970s.

Disco Fever

A more mortifyingly awkward scene you could not hope to concoct: the girls, under the watchful eye of the teachers, go through their dance moves as one shambling line, while the boys look on from the safety of the seats, trying to appear indifferent. And so the formula for a million school discos was set and the division of the world into those who liked to dance (girls) and those who didn't (boys) came about.

The trouble with disco was that nobody taught you how to do it. Unlike the more formal dancing of decades gone by, disco was free-form, spontaneous and therefore prone to horrendous misjudgements. As a result, lots of people chose to watch from the sidelines in the hope of catching an encouraging glance from the one they had their eye on.

This is, in fact, a Saturday morning disco – yes, they actually went into school specially on a Saturday to go through this self-inflicted torture.

Sammy the water-skiing dog and his mistress Deborah enjoy the waters of Torquay seafront on a sunny summer's day. Performing animals were big news in the 1970s, famous examples being Henry the Minced Morsels bloodhound, the PG Tips chimpanzees and a dog called Prince that could say 'sausages'.

A group of boys in their treetop hideout. Playing in the woods was a popular pastime for children in the 1970s. It was a simple and natural pleasure, a local wilderness where you could let your imagination run wild and still be home in time for tea.

If there's one word that sums up the multitude of fashions that came and went during the 1970s, it would have to be flamboyant. A decade that arrived with hippies in Afghan coats and went out with New Romantics dressed like buccaneers,

1970s style

the 1970s took a no-holds-barred approach to style not seen since the court of Louis XIV. Footballers led the way in their shiny polyester shirts, little tight shorts and bubble perms. Take a bow, Gordon Bolland of Millwall (left). The one golden rule that ran like a thread throughout the decade: don't blend into the background. Even the more conventional members of society would at some time have been seen in flared trousers, wing collars and *Planet of the Apes* sideburns.

And then it would all change. The hair would be cut short, the trousers taken in; each trend was a rebellion against the one before. And each fashion had its own musical soundtrack: rock'n'roll, psychedelia, disco, glam rock, prog rock, punk rock, r'n'b, ska, new wave, synthpop, hip-hop, new romantic… The 1970s was a decade of cultural movements, with which young people aligned themselves passionately, wearing their colours with pride, until it was time to swap them for a whole new outfit. As a result, the 1970s saw some of the most ridiculous fashions ever.

Left *A mixture of fashion and marketing: three employees from one of the new breed of computer firms wear flower-power style dresses designed to resemble the look of computer keyboards, on a day out at Ascot races. Even for Ascot, these were unusually eye-catching outfits.*

Right *Actor Peter Wyngarde (aka Jason King, left) parades the sartorial style that earned him the award for Britain's Best Male Personality in 1970, presented to him by the previous year's winner Barry Gibb. Big collars, big cuffs, big tie, big hair, big tache… you get the formula.*

The facial expressions belie the cheerful clothing of these three dejected Newcastle United fans, who have been unable to get a ticket for their team's FA Cup Final against Liverpool and are sitting out the game outside Wembley Stadium. The three roars they heard from Liverpool fans would not have helped their mood.

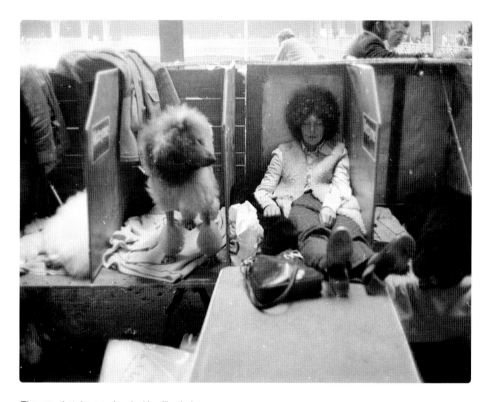

They say that dogs end up looking like their owners.
Or is it the other way round? In this case, the dog has
come along in just the right decade to substantiate the
theory, and while its owner takes a nap, it has its eyes
on the Pup of the Year award at Olympia.

Roaring Success

A popular day out in the 1970s was a trip to a safari park. In 1966, Longleat had opened as the first drive-through safari park outside Africa, and it was followed by Windsor in 1969 and Woburn in 1970. So began the exotic tradition of flirting with rhinos in cars built from wafer-thin tin, sitting for hours with your windows wound up waiting for the lions to wake up, and having the rubber stripped off your windscreen wipers by the baboons.

While there was something incongruous about a pride of lions huddling in a fold of the English countryside on an overcast day in March, the public flocked to the safari parks. Compared to the caged enclosures of the zoos, it was a much more exciting way to see these big beasts, a little taste of what it might be like to see them in the wild. And the threat of one of them trying to break in and grab your jam sandwiches always added a little extra spice to the experience. The animals seemed happier too, especially those baboons.

They may not have lived in mock-Tudor mansions behind electric gates, with personal shoppers and their own fashion brands, but footballers' wives were an enviable bunch even in the 1970s. Here the wives of the Leeds United players assemble before the 1970 FA Cup Final.

Vespa Service

By no means a common sight, even in those days, three nuns from the order of the Little Sisters of the Assumption use stylish scooters to patrol the streets of Edinburgh, attending to the sick among the city's working-class communities. Only one of them is wearing a crash helmet – a freedom of choice enjoyed by all motorcyclists until 1973, when the Motor Cycles (Wearing of Helmets) Act was passed, making it compulsory for a crash helmet to be worn by all riders. Three years later an exemption was admitted to allow members of the Sikh faith to ride without a crash helmet so as not to interfere with their turban. Nuns, however, were not exempt.

The Vespa was a classic Italian scooter popular with the Mods of the 1960s as a style statement against the British motorcycles of their Rocker counterparts. It enjoyed a resurgence in popularity after the 1979 release of the film *Quadrophenia*, a popular classic among Britain's youths, which brought Mod culture back into vogue for a while.

Women of the Year Luncheon 1979

GREATER LONDON FUND FOR

29th Octo

*The age of
permissiveness
had one formidable
opponent: Mary
Whitehouse. Her
campaign against
sex and violence
on television was a
constant thorn in the
side of producers
seeking to reflect the
mood of the time. Here
she is pictured with
American comedienne
Carol Channing (left) at
the Savoy Hotel.*

Dave Hill, guitarist with Slade, on stage at the Hammersmith Odeon. Slade, who had been a skinhead band in the 1960s, reinvented themselves to become the foremost glam rock band of the early 1970s, with a string of hits, including a record three singles that went straight to number one.

*Scottish bad boys
The Bay City Rollers
bridged the gap
between glam rock
and punk and became
the British answer to
American heart throbs
David Cassidy and The
Osmonds. Their glam
yob style and teeny-
bopper pop broke a
million teenage hearts
when they shot to fame
in 1974.*

The neck tie was no longer a simple strip of plain material, it was a garish work of art. Here, ten top tie men, including boxer Henry Cooper (front middle) and future chancellor Norman Lamont (rear, second from right), show off their 'winning' accessories The idea of famous faces selling products was really beginning to get going in the UK.

Doctor at Large

Tom Baker, aka Doctor Who, joins some of the series' famous creations queuing for a visa outside the US Embassy in Grosvenor Square, as the BBC bids to break the show in America.

Doctor Who was essential Saturday evening viewing throughout the 1970s, with first John Pertwee and then Baker bringing their own brand of eccentricity to the title role. Baker remains the longest-serving doctor, having first regenerated into the character in 1974 and continued his travels through time and space until 1981. But the real stars of the show were the monsters, which, for all their lack of technical sophistication, were scary enough to send the nation's youngsters running to hide behind the sofa, returning only to watch through the cracks in their fingers.

In the foreground is K-9, the robot dog that had an encyclopaedic brain and nose-mounted laser. Behind Baker is a dalek, hoping, no doubt, that the US Embassy has a ramp up to the front door.

Fly Me!

Stewardesses from different airlines stand in front of a model of Concorde, looking forward to the day when they will attend to passengers on board the real thing.

Concorde, produced jointly by British Aerospace Corporation and the French Aérospatiale, had first flown in 1969 but did not come into commercial service until 1976. When it was finally launched as a passenger jet, huge crowds turned up at Heathrow to watch its maiden flight.

The plane's sleek styling, though a product of the 1960s, made Concorde a 1970s icon, a symbol of futuristic endeavour. It was the first passenger jet to fly faster than the speed of sound and the noise from its engines was as distinctive as its long, pointy nose. You could always tell when Concorde was coming – the roar hit you in the stomach, which was not universally popular and meant that Concorde's global impact was somewhat curtailed.

For the older members of British society, the styles changed little in the early 1970s. At this working men's club in Newcastle the flat cap, jacket and tie are still very much de rigueur as they congregate to discuss the issues of the day over a pint or two of ale.

Women, as ever, were more receptive to changing fashions. Their hair, their clothes and even their role in society were all constantly on the agenda, and this discussion on a Saturday night out could have been about equal pay or where the woman on the left bought her dress.

Swedish quartet
Abba became the
pop sensation of the
1970s. After winning
the Eurovision Song
Contest in 1974, they
achieved consistent
chart success around
the world for the rest of
the decade and beyond.
Their stage costume
was a singular mix of
glam and disco, that
the public generally
preferred to look at than
to mimic.

Sid Vicious, pursued by his ill-fated girlfriend Nancy Spungen, sports the spiky hair that became the punk rock style in the late 1970s. The dark shirt and thin tie are a kick against the 'hippie' styles that punk sought to replace – or maybe he was due in court.

Left *The popular obsession with a future of hi-tech automation is reflected in this bizarre contraption – a Sumlock adding machine – being demonstrated at the Business Efficiency Exhibition in 1971. For some reason the Sumlock never quite took off – one of countless bright ideas that were too quickly consigned to the dustbin of history.*

Right *Even the simple act of lying in bed became the subject of the Utopian dream. This Sleepcentre from bed maker Slumberland features all mod cons: telephone, TV, radio, allowing the user to live a rich and fulfilling existence without ever having to get out of bed.*

The British motor manufacturing industry was starting to flag in the 1970s, but the Mini remained a popular favourite, boosted by the 1969 release of The Italian Job, *in which the Mini played a starring role. This double-ended version was not available to the public for some reason.*

This policeman, whose uniform has not been influenced by the wide ties and wing collars of the age, manages to avoid the lamp-post but appears oblivious to the man carrying a body over his shoulder. In fact, it's a dummy being used in the 1973 television production of Frankenstein: The True Story.

Members of the religious sect the Children of God go in search of converts on the streets of Brighton. It was a time when disaffected youths went in search of a more spiritual meaning to life, and parents had nightmares about losing their offspring to a wide variety of 'cults'.

A trainload of skinheads disembark at Southend in 1970 to find the police waiting for them. They obligingly stand and listen while the chief inspector lectures them on the correct way to behave during their day at the seaside, including keeping to groups of three or less.

Brighton beach provides a welcome rest for members of ska bands The Specials, Madness and The Selecter, during the 2 Tone tour that got Britain's youth dancing to a different beat. The 2 Tone bands also brought in a new sartorial style, drawing largely from the skinhead fashions of a few years before.

The spirit of peace and love spread to the animal kingdom, with a strong focus on animal cruelty. In this picture, top model Celia Hammond is locked in a cage to raise awareness of an exhibition being staged by the recently formed Compassion in World Farming Trust.

This gorilla at Twycross Zoo may not be roaming free but he has at least got a television in his room. However, it being the 1970s, he's discovered that watching daytime television means gazing at the BBC test card for hours on end.

The age of the daredevil motorcyclist saw Britain's very own Eddie Kidd emerge in response to the bus-jumping feats of America's Evel Knievel. Here Kidd attempts to become the first man to jump ten Radio One disc jockeys on a motorcycle. Sadly, he cleared them all.

John Lydon (aka Johnny Rotten) and Steve Jones of the Sex Pistols perform a benefit gig in Huddersfield for the children of striking firefighters on Christmas Day, 1977. An alternative to the Queen's Speech at the end of Jubilee year, it was a last English hurrah for the band who split up the following month.

A way of life

The 1970s was a decade of extremes. The British character had evolved since the Second World War, through discipline and austerity to an age of liberation and self-expression. People weren't just going to do what they were told any more; a mindset that produced political and social conflict in parallel with an unselfconscious joie de vivre. In short, the British people had become less buttoned up and the man in the pin-striped suit and bowler hat was now a figure of fun.

Television and radio had given the nation new role models, comedians like the Goons with a keen sense of the absurd, whose example was followed in the 1970s by *Monty Python's Flying Circus*. Being silly was a proud part of the national psyche: when all else failed, we pulled a funny face.

These two are contestants in no less than the World Gurning Championship – a contest that attracted little competition from abroad – held on this occasion against the glamorous backdrop of the Egremont Crab Fair in Cumberland. A far cry from the Miss World pageant, yet somehow far more relevant to the British way of life.

Some demonstrations were more popular than others. However, many Britons did still regard themselves as distinct from other Europeans and were averse to seeing that distinction eroded via political manoeuvres like forging closer economic ties with Europe. In 1972, they lost their battle and Britain joined the Common Market.

Some traditions were still going strong, such as the annual pancake race taking place in communities all over Britain on Shrove Tuesday. This contestant has opted for a very small pan, yet the pancake still appears to have escaped her and is on its way earthwards.

Festival-goers at the first 'Glastonbury Fair' in 1971 form a circle to perform some form of druid-style ceremony. Worthy Farm had hosted its first music festival the previous year, named The Pilton Pop, Blues and Folk Festival, inspired by the Isle of Wight Festival and other open-air concerts.
Acts this time around included Hawkwind, David Bowie, Traffic, Joan Baez and Fairport Convention, it was free to get in and 12,000 attended.

Football fans on a packed terrace at Highbury, the home of Arsenal,
look on as a yobbo is ejected from the ground by a member of the
constabulary before kick-off against Manchester United. This was the first
day of the season that would see United, European champions five years
earlier, get relegated.

*A classic stereotype and inspiration for countless comedy sketches:
the British businessman – or four of them in this case – napping on the
London Underground after another gruelling day at work. The charcoal
suit, the furled umbrella, the briefcase and the bowler hat are all there. All
that's missing is* The Times *crossword.*

The 1970s was a golden age for UK TV. The Professionals *(above) starred Martin Shaw, Gordon Jackson and Lewis Collins as agents of the fictional CI5. Other popular shows of the decade were* The Sweeney, The Muppet Show, Rising Damp, Starsky and Hutch, Some Mothers Do 'Ave 'Em, Citizen Smith, Kojak, Fawlty Towers… *the list goes on and on.*

Leaders of the Greek Orthodox Church in Margate, where there is a large Greek-Cypriot community, are joined by clergymen from the Church of England and the Roman Catholic Church for the annual Blessing of the Sea ceremony, a Greek Orthodox tradition that came to England in the 1960s.

A fascinating portrait of couples sitting in Trafalgar Square: the people-watchers watched. They're all smartly dressed, apart from the young man with his foot up on the bench, and most of them seem to be lost in their own thoughts as they wait for whatever it is they're waiting for.

A milkman about to deliver someone their breakfast of milk, corn flakes and a loaf of bread. Electric milk floats were a common sight on Britain's roads in the 1970s and if you asked nicely the milkman would give you a ride up the road and might even let you drive.

A couple from London soak up the sun on a day out in Southend. Big group outings to the seaside were becoming less common, with most families having their own private car and planning their own excursions when they felt like it. Some even eschewed the British resort for warmer climes.

The sight of girls becoming hysterical at the sight of pop stars hadn't ended with The Beatles. Here distraught girlfriends console one another in the aftermath of a brief appearance by The Osmonds on the balcony of a hotel in London – enough to provoke heartbreak, trauma and floods of tears.

Hop pickers from London go about their work in the fields of Kent. The annual hop harvest brought an exodus of whole families from the capital to spend a few days of summer bringing in the crop to ensure a bountiful supply of beer, which they would then spend the evenings drinking.

Sir Freddie Laker opened up a whole new world of holiday destinations for average Britons when he launched his pioneering, low-cost Laker Airways in 1973. Here he sits on the runway at Gatwick Airport, waiting for the inaugural flight of his Skytrain.

Race Relations

Members of an Afro-Caribbean church group hold a meeting in Derby town centre. Britain's white population were still struggling to come to terms with the growing number of black and Asian people in their neighbourhoods, while black people were growing tired of the discrimination to which they were constantly subjected.

While the first generation of Afro-Caribbean and Asian immigrants had taken the casual racism on the chin, their children were now old enough to fight back. The latter end of the decade was marred by regular clashes between blacks, police, the National Front and anti-racist groups.

The sitcom *Love Thy Neighbour* tried to hold a mirror up to the absurdity of the situation: white Englanders coming to terms with having black neighbours – the wives integrating happily, the husbands constantly at loggerheads. But in reality, it was no laughing matter.

Seaside postcard humour was at its peak, thanks largely to the Carry On films, featuring comedy actors like Kenneth Williams, Charles Hawtry, Sid James and Hattie Jacques. Here Hawtry and Williams pursue actress Patsy Rowlands on Brighton Pier during the filming of Carry On At Your Convenience.

Left *The 1970s saw some scorching summers, particularly in 1976 and 1977, when the country was hit by a severe drought, spawning the humorous slogan: 'Save Water, Bath with a Friend'. For most Brits it was a welcome chance to get outdoors and soak up some rays, preferably while being pampered.*

Right *Not quite Vegas, the amusement arcade here amounts to little more than a few one-armed bandits plugged into the wall. All the amusements were mechanical and offered the promise of a pocketful of coppers if you were lucky. Not life-changing but still strangely irresistible.*

In 1977 the nation developed a passion for pageantry. The Queen's Silver Jubilee rekindled a community spirit virtually forgotten since her Coronation and as the sun shone on the parades and the street parties, there was a palpable sense of people feeling proud to be British.

*On the streets of Belfast, the mood wasn't quite so jolly.
The constant presence of British troops provoked regular
hostilities from local youths, which in turn prompted often
brutal retaliation. The cycle of violence in Northern Ireland
was a depressing fact of life in the 1970s.*

One of the most divisive aspects of life was race – or rather your attitude to race. The power to stop and search caused an explosive tension between the police and the Afro-Caribbean population, which occasionally boiled over into open conflict, such as this riot at the Notting Hill Carnival in 1976.

Left *Fans of Elvis Presley look soberly at their prayer sheets during a memorial service for the American 'King of Rock'n'Roll', who died in 1977 at the age of 42. A fortnight after his death, eight of his hit singles were re-released in Britain, all entering the Top 50.*

Right *The shape of things to come. Conservative Party leader Margaret Thatcher, who would end the decade as Britain's first woman prime minister and remain in power throughout the 1980s, watches a 16-year-old William Hague, later to lead the party himself, speaking at the Conservative Party Conference in 1977.*

Children of the 1970s –
where are they now?